Volume 83 of the Yale Series of Younger Poets

To the
Place of
Trumpets

Brigit Pegeen Kelly

Foreword by James Merrill

Yale University Press
New Haven and London

Publication of this volume was made possible
by a gift from The Guinzburg Fund.

Designed by Sally Harris
and set in Garamond type by
Brevis Press, Bethany, Connecticut.
Printed in the United States of America

Library of Congress Cataloging-in-Publication Data

Kelly, Brigit Pegeen, 1951–
    To the place of trumpets / Brigit Pegeen Kelly;
foreword by James Merrill.
        p.   cm.—(Yale series of younger poets:
v. 83)
    ISBN 978-0-300-04151-4

    I. Title.   II. Series.
PS3561.E3927T6   1988
811'.54—dc19   87-26570
                        CIP

The paper in this book meets the guidelines for
permanence and durability of the Committee on
Production Guidelines for Book Longevity of the
Council on Library Resources.

for my family

Contents

Foreword   *ix*
Acknowledgments *xiii*

Part I

After Your Nap   *3*
Music School   *4*
The Greek Alphabet   *5*
Doing Laundry on Sunday   *7*
Sundays   *9*
Near the Race Track   *13*
Spring Musical, Harmony School   *14*
Queen Elizabeth and the Blind Girl *or*
    Music for the Dead Children   *16*
The Peaceable Kingdom   *19*

Part II

Harmony Stoneworks, Late Winter   *23*
The Thief's Wife   *24*
Garden Among Tombs   *26*
Dog   *28*
Young Wife's Lament   *30*
The Cruel Mother   *32*
The White Deer   *35*

Part III

The Teacher   *39*
Imagining Their Own Hymns   *40*
The Leaving   *42*
Napa Valley   *43*
Mount Angel   *45*
Christmas Eve, Old People's Guild, Mt. Angel   *46*
The Hill   *48*
The House on Main Street   *50*

Part IV

Those Who Wrestle With the Angel For Us   57
Given the River   59
Above the Quarry   60
The Visitation   62
The Place of Trumpets   64
To the Lost Child   66
Lullaby for the Gardener   69

"Man is only man superficially," wrote Valéry. "Remove his skin, dissect, and at once you come to machinery." True enough; and cutting through the surface of personal experience, you arrive at a realm of myth, archetype, fable, and metaphor—machinery of the sort in which a god descends. Here, oddly enough, we are more often at home than in the world of fact. Only a specialist, a pilot for instance, or an engineer, lives by his knowledge that the earth is round. The rest of us daily make do with an old wives' tale.

But "make do" hardly describes Brigit Pegeen Kelly's exuberant ways with words. At the simplest level she retains the wild, transforming eye of childhood. "Sundays" evokes that stage when names are just beginning to stick to their referents, and "Mr. Fudd" is as delicious to utter as "red" or "rabbit." When Anna's husband, in his church-going best, smiles

> his head comes forward
> and his teeth come forward
> as if he brought his fence out farther
> to make the yard larger
> to let more people in.

To *take* more people in, the grown-up poet might say, but slyness is out of place in this child's drawing. The same poem gives us "red trees, ruby grass, crimson sun," like some primal orgy with a box of crayons. Such effects grow subtler as her personae mature, but Kelly never abandons color as a virtual myth in itself, the way it is in Stevens or Chagall.

Many poems reflect her Catholic background. A lapsed Episcopalian, I can both marvel at my narrow escape and catch myself sighing in retrospect for the deeper dyes and forcefuller early imprint of Rome. We tend to think that any religious education has its drawbacks—a warped view of history, say, or of science— yet here in Protestant America, whose children are raised believing that nothing is truly intricate or miraculous, and no longer know even the stories of Aesop and Grimm, let alone Bulfinch and the Bible, to have been partly educated by nuns or rabbis or the imam at the mosque downtown is a distinct advantage. You enter college, as it were, on a scholarship of which your smiling WASP classmates have been pitifully deprived.

In Kelly's work the Catholic heritage will be transmuted beyond any taint of dogma. First, though, she must escape. One angry poem has a little girl focusing her rebellion through figures in the stained-glass church windows:

> When the sun comes up behind the angels
> then even in their dun robes they are beautiful,
> with their girlish hair and their mean lit faces,
> but they do not love the light. As I
> do not love it when I am made clean
> for the ladies who bring my family money.

The angels are "sick of Jesus, / who never stops dying," thinks the child, and "One night they will get out of here . . ."

> together, as in a wedding march,
> their pockets full of money from the boxes
> for the sick poor, they will walk down the aisle,
> imagining their own hymns . . .

Rebel angels—like the child, sick of the sweetness and light she is made to embody. Those last four words give this poem its title, and reading further we understand that to imagine her own hymns after leaving church is the project (again Stevens comes to mind) for all of Kelly's poetry to date. Most ominous here is the falsification inflicted upon the child for appearances' sake. In "Queen Elizabeth and the Blind Girl," so as not to forgo the gift brought by its royal godmother, a dead infant is rouged into the semblance of sleep. The deception sets off a toccata for deaf bell-ringer and a shopful of talking birds. Fairy-tale touches like these repeatedly work their counterspell. Through them—linked as they are with necessities ("money . . . for the sick poor")—Kelly does considerable justice to the Church's hold upon her young life, and to the cost at which she struggles free of it.

Free of the shaping past? Isn't the most we can do, to be free
with it, submit it to some shaping of our own? This freedom, in
any case, I find especially heartening in Kelly's poems. Far from
leading to negation or bitterness, her lost faith becomes the stuff
of vision. She fabulizes, she distances. The Mount Angel poems
depict a community grown simpleminded, even bucolic. The
priest's sermon "was nothing to me,"

> so sure was I of the crown
> of rain falling over the flowers, the stone
> benches, the fields far below where the Old
> Believers, haloed with strawberry moths, bent
> and picked fruit . . .

Here the language of transcendence is deflected onto the landscape
surrounding the monastery, and given the lightest possible coup
de grâce by those haloes of moths. In a landscape more idyllic
yet flow streams "over whose waters / the sun passes like a silver
hand carrying a cup of wine," an image as ecstatic as any in the
Song of Songs. Elsewhere a bull named Moses "all improbably"
eats a burning bush. Or (in "Garden Among Tombs") a soldier
who sleeps through the Resurrection tells on waking not that
Judas's palm but that his, the sleeper's, own legs have been
"crossed . . . with silver" by the passage of nocturnal snails.
Kelly's imagination breeds heresies as innocent and plentiful as
mayflies. Thanks to it we can feel this Christian story—which
has weighed so painfully upon the world for centuries—at last
breaking down, granite to schist, leaving only the odd recalci-
trance of a phrase or the fractured mica-flash of an ancient image.

Thus delivered, Kelly writes some of her best poems. One of
them ("Those Who Wrestle With the Angel For Us") tells how
her brother, now an aviator, as a little boy

> dragged a stick along the fence rails, and listened
> To the slatted rattle of the railroad cars, and knew by

> Instinct how railroad lines look from the air, like ladders
> Running northward to the stars, to the great constellations.

And he began then tracking his way through the names
Of all our fears, Cassiopeia, Andromeda, the shining Ram,

Tracking the miles and years he logs now . . .

We hear the stick echo the railroad cars, see rails and cross-ties
form the upraised ladder, feel cars merging with stars, and tracks
with the young star-gazer's tracking eye. These are lines finely
conceived and written. For all its plainer language "The House
on Main Street" ends upon a note no less exalted—which sug-
gests, too, where some of those renegade angels may presently be
glimpsed. The poet and her daughter, collecting feathers in the
cemetery they've been using as a playground, imagine themselves

connected with flight, not with the stone angels
    shadowing the frozen
        ground, but with a body
that has truly flown, with a mind
    that makes the sky
    its home.

With this poem Brigit Pegeen Kelly casts a wide descriptive net,
in the manner of Marianne Moore's "The Steeple-Jack," over a
townscape with figures. The occasion, "a funeral to which I was
not / invited," gives her lavish access to the world of fact: the
full church with "the whole town . . . singing / inside"; a recent
case of arson; hydrangeas withered (by their abuse in a previous
poem?); a bag of clothespins "like a wasps' nest"; a murdered
girl. The scene comes to life through the eyes of the poet, who—
nostalgic for a home left far behind, but easy in her present,
somewhat 'Aquarian' way of life—includes herself among the local
oddballs. No, not quite: she has settled on a nearby hill, reluc-
tantly but significantly above them all.

James Merrill

Acknowledgments

Grateful acknowledgment is made to the following publications in which these poems, or versions of these poems, first appeared or are forthcoming.

The Anthology of Eugene Writers #1: "After Your Nap"

Anthology of Magazine Verse and Yearbook of American Poetry: "Mount Angel"

Creeping Bent: "The Hill"; "Near the Race Track"

The Georgia Review: "Those Who Wrestle With the Angel For Us"

Ironwood: "Above the Quarry"; "Dog"

The Nation: "Young Wife's Lament"

New England Review and Bread Loaf Quarterly: "Imagining Their Own Hymns"

Northwest Review: "Given the River"; "Harmony Stoneworks, Late Winter"; "Spring Musical, Harmony School"; "Sundays"; "To the Lost Child"

Poetry: "Doing Laundry on Sunday"; "Mount Angel"; "Napa Valley"

Poetry Northwest: "Christmas Eve, Old People's Guild, Mt. Angel"; "Garden Among Tombs"; "The Greek Alphabet"; "The Peaceable Kingdom"; "The Thief's Wife"

Prairie Schooner: "The Leaving"; "Queen Elizabeth and the Blind Girl *or* Music for the Dead Children"

Quarry West: "Music School"

Saint Andrews Review: "the pool" (from "The Cruel Mother")

Sweet Reason: "After Your Nap"

West Branch: "The Teacher"; "The Visitation"; "The White Deer"

I would like to thank the National Endowment for the Arts and the New Jersey State Council on the Arts for grants that helped me in writing this book. Special thanks also to Maxine Scates, Michelle Piso, Laurie George, Rich Wyatt, Michael Madonick, and my parents, Gretta and Robert Glynn Kelly, for their patient assistance and encouragement.

Part I

After Your Nap

(for Maria)

I carry you outside
and we sit on the porch,

before us the vast expanse of bee-studded lawn
and the blank pastel shingle of the housing opposite.

In an upstairs window the dim t-shirt of a man moves,
is swallowed, returns again from shadow—a buoy

indolently bobbing on a gray and mild sea.
You roll away from me and lie on your back,

the small sack of your body filling slowly with itself,
while children careen and call

and I cradle my marriage gently in my lap—
a quiet thing, small, a thing barely breathing,

like those curtains rising so faintly opposite
that could at any moment become taut, full-bellied

or fall to utter stillness.
The sky is ash colored, purple to the North—

they are burning grass from the fields.
The light is growing loose, the way clothes do

after having been worn for a long time.
In wide banded circles the birds rise and fall.

I run my hand over the neat purse of your small belly
the hard knot of your pubis

and think how surely we are contained
how well our small boundaries love us.

Music School

All day long the birds lounge
on the rotting plush of the rose bush,
drunk on the rancid scent,
and play and play on their dime store instruments.
They practice so hard and never get it right.
I pound the wall but they will not stop.
They think that the whole world is chortling.
They think that my pounding is the beat of their tiny hearts.
They are dazed by the sun that presses its belly against them,
convincing them that they are their songs
and that they will never again inhabit their shabby bodies.

The Greek Alphabet

(for Christine Psathas)

It is not true
that my four-year-old brother cut all the
curls from Anthony's Greek head and hid them
under the mulberry bush and that your mother
would not speak to my mother for weeks, but
sat brooding over espresso, while Anthony,
indifferent to his patched scalp, burbled
like a canary and bobbed biscuits in his
sweetened half cup.
                         Nor is it true that
at night on birthdays the hushed willows
leaned in and the dining room's beamed
ceiling rose, candles fanning the circle of
moon faces, your mother singing in Greek,
spinning the black powdered cake full of
dimes like a roulette wheel, to bring the
birthday child blessing—the hard sound
of the horn.
                    Your house burned, Christine,
the year after you had gone North to the sea
and to your new friend Suki who was special
because she had lost all her teeth, the same
year that Nina Raia was shot by her lover in
the schoolyard (and Mr. Raia in his suit on
his knees planted tulip bulbs all over the
lawn), the year that gangs of boys stripped
all the fruit from the neighborhood trees
and dumped it into the ravine to rot; on a
Sunday night, while the Baptists sang and
the firemen's hose leapt like a schoolgirl's
jumprope, in clouds of ruby smoke, your house
burned; and I stood barefoot, in my flannel
pajamas, watching the huge brass-footed
bathtub—the best thing in your house, the

tub that was always full of scalding water
and amber both oil, the tub around which you
had danced, naked, draped in your mother's
veil, your dark hands gathering steam as if
it were wheat—blackening in orange flame,
while dumb George shuffled up and down Clark
Street pounding his pail and muttering doom,
and the bells of St. Bartholomew's softly
boomed . . .

                                        Christine,
none of this is true, but each Spring in the
Raias' yard, red and yellow tulips tumble in
the blowing grass, and Roberta wades among
them, lopping their heads off and stuffing
them in her purse.

Doing Laundry on Sunday

So this is the Sabbath, the stillness
in the garden, magnolia
bells drying damp petticoats

over the porch rail, while bicycle
wheels thrum and the full-breasted tulips
open their pink blouses

for the hands that pressed them first
as bulbs into the earth.
Bread, too, cools on the sill,

and finches scatter bees
by the Shell Station where a boy
in blue denim watches oil

spread in phosphorescent scarves
over the cement. He dips
his brush into a bucket and begins

to scrub, making slow circles
and stopping to splash water on the children
who, hours before it opens,

juggle bean bags outside Gantsy's
Ice Cream Parlor,
while they wait for color to drench their tongues,

as I wait for water to bloom
behind me—white foam, as of magnolias,
as of green and yellow

birds bathing in leaves—wait,
as always, for the day, like bread, to rise
and, with movement

imperceptible, accomplish everything.

Sundays

i.

Under the black walnuts on the church lawn,
Anna wears her face
like a new hat. The sweet smell
of rosewater, the smell
of restoration, the smell of skin
dreaming of finery and better
people all around.

> Blood is red and
> the lips. And light
> is blue, and the eyelids.
> And milk is white
> and the neck.

And over her shoulders the beautiful
nubbed shawl, gray as doves'
bellies all together, or the rose-noted
dove's song, or the priest's
Irish vowels.

And her husband's teeth
are whale-bone
perfect, a wrist band hoop, tight
and right and singing
of seas and salt. And when he smiles
his head comes forward
and his teeth come forward
as if he brought his fence out farther
to make the yard larger
to let more people in.

ii.

Rabbits have teeth and feet
and Mr. Fudd after them
fat as gum. It is hard to be a hunter,
over and over, always the kite
snagged in the tree, always the balloon
just out of reach.

Always to be caught in Sam's broken t.v.
under the dimestore counter. Weasel or Fudd
it is hard to see red—
red trees, ruby grass, crimson sun.

And the shelves sigh like pews.
They are weary of news, they are weary
of feet and toothpaste and glue.

And the people are weary of Sam, who
never looks up,
but feels for your money with his hand.
You could stand at his door and call
Roses have come! Roses have come!
but he'd only send out the blind dog.

And the cash register bangs gold.
And Elmer's gun bangs red.
And the door to the store bangs black.
And talcum settles
like incense over the polished wood floor.

iii.

A clown has feet of another color,
has hands as feet,
my monkey with his heels
over his head, swinging from Mr. Morgan's
sycamores.

He is the pendulum of a clock
gone wrong, or the off-key song
in Mr. Morgan's head, or
the gun in his lap that shines
in the sun. Like the licorice Lorraine
threw up in the jewelry store
all over the velvet
and the stones.

And the jays play Fly Away Peter
Fly Away Paul, and they do.
And the sycamores dance Ring Around
the Moon and drop their skins
in puddles at our feet.

And the sky says that
the house of hate has close walls
and hands over the eyes
not to see my monkey cross the lawn
not to see
Mr. Morgan drop his gun and run
not to see
them both together call. Bird calls
and man calls
and calls that are not,
cats-eating-tin calls,
the calls of martins in flight,
calls that roll orange groves out in the night,
that fill the musk deer with mercy
and the lion with fury,
that stand trees
up like shots on the lawn
and snow crows from the clouds down,

calls like piccolos, or mouth organs,
or beautiful gold pipes
that bring milk to our ears, or words,

our mothers, our names,

what wakes us where we sleep.

iv.

And the lost calf—little
lily-breathed, tufted-bird-feather
furred—is now in the field,
with the bigger cows nosing him
and the Rose of Sharon dropping
pink bathwater
all down his back.

He is small, not yet into his horns
and his heels, knowing
nothing but the sun,
and the dying thistle,
and the field that has come back

and is best.

Near the Race Track

(for Michael)

You will remember the ice cream store,
rising where you did not expect it.
You were stabbing the air with your umbrella
and cursing, you looked up
and in one breath moved into your tongue.
                    Joy is more than a pause.
It is the day swelling like a balloon,
like the hundred hot air balloons
you saw by the race track: cars stalled
on the highway—no police anywhere—

and all that silence rising.

Joy can be made out of cloth and heated
with gas. It can ascend from our hands
and halt us in our shoes. We
can have too few mouths to hold it—
we can be lost in the middle of the day,
by the highway, in the heat.

Spring Musical, Harmony School

(Song for Brother John)

Robin watches the voice rise,
rise like a kite from the girl, rise
and tangle in the streamers above. She laughs
and claps her hands. Slow Robin, rocking
in her folding chair, white-haired Robin staring
at me with that one wild eye, and flapping her arms
as if to fly above us all—the principal
with his limp toupee, the boy knocking spit
from his French horn, the black-capped
conductor and her ivory cane.

Heap damp flowers on the stage!
A sadness sweet as cinnamon hangs in the air.
We will not be here next year to watch
the scrubbed and licked, milk-bathed children
gleam under the streamers and the lights
as they sing to the sleeping Brother: *Wake, John,
wake, the bells are ringing,* the band is beating
fit to kill, and God, God is always waiting
for the slow—Slow Robin, Slow John, the milky
sunlit slowness of childhood—*ding, dang, dong* . . .

—O dear dead Brother, rocking on the earth's
dark waves, angels and swans fanning your
bones, I slept one afternoon by your stone
while sheep grazed under the old oak—such a
sleep, heady with the scent of jasmine and heat,
with the cicadas' spiralling hum, such a sleep
as you must sleep, sung in by children
and circled with small feet. *Sonnez*—listen—
les matines—sweet sound. And time clinks in
its golden chains as the floral curtain

starts to fall over a frail girl
in a faded uniform fighting the last notes
from her tarnished flute, over
a boy who clicks his heels and cocks his head
like our bull calf, Moses, tender and wild—over
Robin rocking the child she will never have.
—Dear dead Brother, hammocked the world
over in the cupped palms of a thousand, thousand,
balm-carrying voices, why should you wake?
Sleep. Sleep. The world will wait.

Queen Elizabeth and the Blind Girl or Music for the Dead Children

The Queen sneezed at Helmingham. The chapel
was cold. The incense bad. Outside rooks screamed
among the stones. And though the Queen did not
    know it—so sweetly Mrs. Tollemache rocked
    the child, so brightly its rouged lips shone—

Elizabeth's godson was two days dead.
A harmless deception. Who would begrudge
the Tollemaches their day of grace, the flurries
    of the false baptismal bells, the flurries
    of spring snow, candlelight on the Queen's

carnelian hair? In the tapestried hall
partridges dropped golden grease, a jester
shrieked, black and white robed singers opened their
    moist mouths in perfect halos of sound, and
    on the carved table before the fire—

as Elizabeth at last rode out that
day in 1578 under
the winged stone horses—lay the Queen's gift to her
    godson, a Rose lute, glistening like a new moon
    or the wet beak of a parrot.

*   *   *   *   *

Today the blind girl is burying her
boy in Saint Bartholomew's yard. She kneels
in the warm snow, crushing crocuses
    beneath her dark kilt, while across the street a boy,
    singing *man-O man-O man-O man,*

drags his clattering stick along the iron
fence rails. The blind girl looks up. The whole grave
party with her looks up, but the boy
     doesn't notice. He is a conductor.
     His limbs leap like warm marigolds. The fence

rails are people. They clap. They clap. *O fine*
they say *O fine fine fine* and the whole sky
wings down. Just so, a woman will lean from
     her window and cry *fire!* and the red trucks
     will come flying, bringing bare feet clapping

on the cold sidewalk before the flames, and the
watery clang of the bells that wake all
sleepers, as now Saint Bartholomew's bells
     wake the slumbering birds in their hot shop
     beneath the copper roof, one dead bell

knocking among three that are still alive,
rolling in their tower—that old stone ear
full of remembered sound and the soot-stained
     flackering wings of the steeple's white doves.
     The bell ringer is deaf! The maker

of sound is deaf! And because he thinks
of the past—(The past, too, is a dove.
She is tired of the tower. There are
     too many prisoners. There is too little
     sky. She knows the winged horses

will never fly)—he rings not the death bells
but the baptismal bells. And he wishes
for the blind girl not sight but the bird shop.
     Wishes that one afternoon, there in the
     heat under the elephantine vines,

the cockatoo, milky as a tame
rabbit, will lift for her its plume and sigh.
Sigh like a hundred piano keys
    yellowing. Sigh like the softly spinning
    wheels of old clocks. Sigh amid the xylophone

rattle of three rooms of stacked cages,
shrieks and cries, beaks splitting wood, lovebirds
somersaulting beneath the loose senegals
    whose wide wings beat the wall, and in the center
    of it all, on his red perch, the giant

blue macaw swinging his beak against
the white brazil nut meat: *chuff, chuff, wind the clocks,*
my dear, time for tea, time for tunes, time
    will come round and fountain as my feathers do
    into glorious dust mops, bloom

like hydrangeas, and, one by one,
as the music box drops its sprung notes
into the pool, all will be well.
    For her he wishes this. For her deft hand
    this. This or what now—as he slowly

rises and falls—he sees far below
his stone tower on the shadowy
snow-patched ground: the many waxwings, juniper
    berries flashing in their beaks, as they wake
    like a hundred green candles in a field.

The Peaceable Kingdom

The leopard is mine, the snow leopard with the face
like a dinner plate, and I am the boy in blue knickers

staring as fiercely as any warrior in any sheepskin
ever stared, but I have no arrows and my leopard will scare

no one. Now, there are only the tulips and the swans unfolding
their soft wings, and the green stream along whose banks

harps are strung in the acacias, over whose waters
the sun passes like a silver hand carrying a cup of wine.

I had not thought enough of death, of entering the black canal,
of rising from the water with my black feathers wet

and my ears open—like the mouths of babes for milk—to drums
and cymbals, gongs and horns, and that song the stars

sing just before dawn, where there is a night for them
to leave behind and the loss of it growing. Now our hearts

are lions' hearts, golden in our breasts, and if we spit
it is Solomon and the silver of all his temples. Not Solomon

Grundy. Nothing is Grundy here. And though my sandals
do not quite fit, and though the little gray lambs will never

leave me alone, there is only *Good morning* in all this,
and *How do you do? And how do you do again?* My mind

is like the harp strings, with a breeze blowing always
and no rest in sight. It is a mind that belongs

to the four winds, and a body that is only the thought of a thought,
a reminder of something the mind tries to gather into a pile

like wheat, but the pile blows away, and I watch gold fragments
turning on the wind. Here the lilies lie down at your feet.

Here everyone wins the prize so you don't know where to look,
whose elbow to softly touch. And there is always

in this liquid air the song my mother sang to me, but now
it is for everyone and my heart, which is a lion's heart,

no longer rolls over and weeps at the sound. What I
wished for is not as I understood it to be, I have still

not seen an angel, unless that red cloud passing beyond the trees
when my leopard went for a walk was one. And though

there are no gates here, no locks or keys, there is also no way
to leave—no way in this lion's heart to desire to do so.

Part II

Harmony Stoneworks, Late Winter

Sunday is silence in the pit, the gate locked,
the trucks gone, the road all mine, mine the stone wall

I sit upon that borders the field, tree-locked
and locked within a larger field. This is where

the spaniel comes, where the alleys of stubble fill
with darkness and wash him toward me—one-eyed spaniel,

filthy, wearing his patched body like a madman's coat
as he runs up one side of the wall and down the other.

Why does he cross this field of stones and cold, of
sodden cobs the reaper dropped, where the hackberries

wrestle to bring forth new leaves? Why does he run
this ring around me? O spaniel, mad spaniel,

are you lost to the whistle, wet in your master's mouth,
too high-pitched or too remote for my ears, calling you

North, calling you South? Or lost to your small heart
telling you cross, cross space and you will own it?

The swallows build the bank. Are you my fear?
Blind as the wind that works to pull their nests down?

The Thief's Wife

He took things and that was bad, but it also
made me feel pleasure, as when we lay by the lake
and he did things to me in broad daylight
that should not have been done, people walking
arm in arm below who must have seen, but I,
stunned with heat, keeping my eyes shut, thinking
that the world when my eyes were shut
was a world that would forgive those who could not see;
or when, another time, he told me he had slept
years before with his sister, thieving even then,
and suddenly that which I could not have imagined
was mine, hundreds of blackbirds massing
in the air outside my door, and he afraid
I would walk away, but I drawn even more toward
that body which made another body lie down
in darkness under it and die. When you are weak
those who walk with evil and live look strong
to you. And if that which was to be your strength
fails you, you will take strength where you can.
And then there were the things. They were so beautiful.
The axes he sharpened and hung over the fence,
their blades like ships' flags, the sky sailing
over them as over water, raising waves of light, and
the hammers and nails with their fine biting sounds,
and rolls of chicken wire stretched in sagging rows
that the honeysuckle spiralled over
in the summer, and the bellies of the pigs, soft
as butter, and the eraser blue spots
beneath the rabbits' ears, and baskets of fruit
which grew pungent as it spoiled, and candy
in gold papers and scotch in swollen-necked bottles,
and needles and pins, and the silk he brought
me once for my birthday, yards of gray silk,

yards of it, lovely as the herons dropping
on wide wings over the lake. I used those things,
saying This is bad, but using them nonetheless.
I never took anything myself, but what is
the difference? Your hand passes over something
that is stolen and settles on it—the way
chicken feathers settled this morning in the honey
I spilled on the table—and then forever
your hand is one with that thing, forever that thing
is in your room. That is why people steal, I think.
To make things last.

A woman with bibles comes to visit me.
Each time she brings a different man in a shiny
brown suit, and each time I let them in, though at night
I dream that they all become beetles
in my yard, swarming in their slick shells, and no way
to put them out. Still, when a poor woman comes
I give her soup, even if my son
strikes me—we will have more where that came from—
and I feed the dogs in the alley since
my own son is a dog, and sometimes I laugh
when I look up at the clock face of the moon
and think that at least my husband wasn't able
to steal that, for if he had, I would have put my hands
all over it—and never let it go.

Garden Among Tombs

(for Julia)

The irises the soldiers are bedded in
are stars. How true
this is they do not know, how deep
and out of their hands
this sleep that came on sandaled feet
softly over stones, that came
with the hushed bounds of leaping
gazelles. Though

they hear, as it were, over
their shoulders, something rising,
like a winged cypress
or a man with his arms arched as if to dive
off the edge of this flat earth
into the red lake, the sky,

and they hear a low humming, blue-
green, as of damselflies
mating over summer water
or lyre strings beneath a girl's fingers

when the soldiers have not seen
a woman for a long time. They hear, too,
skirts in the bushes and a stone
being moved with a great
sigh. Like a thought finally come clear,
or the house free at last from fire—
the sigh of water not needed
anymore, of the sky, as the stars retire,
resting from its watch.

One soldier sleeps with his eyes
half open and his forehead to his knees
as if he looks over water and sees
not his own face
but more—winged hands, and heads like tamarisks
shining in the lake, animals
he does not know with purple legs and silver
fins tangled in kelp, and,
in the middle of it all, a tree
veering like an arm
swathed in layers of red cloth
holding a bouquet of flowers, of feathers,
of leaves with peacocks' eyes
out to an impossible girl.

Later, when he is punished for this sleep
he could not help
he will be glad anyway
that it came, that the snails crossed
his legs with silver,
while the smell of orchids and the smell
of tulips linked hands
and wove something thicker even
than the linen cloth
the people will press their faces against—
as if it holds the impress
of the heavens,
or their own bodies.

Dog

When you first felt the foul dog walking
up the corn row of your spine, you remembered
walking by the soy fields down the long road
to the limestone quarry, remembered the trucks
lumbering and how the mind shut its gates
and called down a sort of sleep to keep
the trucks' roar back. You rode that sound
without resistance, like a boat upon
the working waves, while as each diesel passed
the dog leapt and fought like a fish on the chain
by your side.
          What walks inside walks outside.
Death has a thousand pictures in the world.
You lie and worms eat the oak, you steal
bread and an old woman riddled with
superstitions drops her mirror and weakens
to the loss of luck. There was another dog.
The gentle mongrel given to you
as a gift and hit one day by a truck.
It died slowly on a heap of rags in the shed,
its back legs crushed, soiling itself
as it tried to rise, and howling, howling.
There was the smell of urine and cold cement,
of winter trees and of the snow
that the wind carried in as a biting spray,
while the birds dropped their calls
in the woods. And because the smells
frightened you and the way the dog threw back
his head and would not listen, and how
his eyes, yellowed with pain, would not see,
and how in his head as he cried he went on
walking, walking, wherever it was he walked,
you kicked him to stop the noise,

kicked and kicked, as if you were kicking
the loud wheel of the truck that struck him,
as if you were that wheel itself, raising
a churning wave of snow and then,
like time, rolling over the hill
and never coming back.
                              The dog died.
You ate your meals and said your prayers.
Your life was a life. But now where you sit
at your desk overlooking the wet fields
something scratches at the base of your neck
and pulls your head up, so that you see coming
toward you with dead calm through the dusk
a forest—dark and limbless.

Young Wife's Lament

The mule that lived on the road
where I was married
would bray to wake the morning,
but could not wake me.
How many summers I slept
lost in my hair. How many
mules on how many hills singing.
Back of a deep ravine
he lived, above a small river
on a beaten patch of land.
I walked up in the day and walked down,
having been given nothing
else to do. The road grew no longer,
I grew no wiser, my husband
was away selling things to people who buy.
He went up the road, too, but
the road was full of doors for him,
the road was his belt and,
one notch at a time, he loosened it
on his way. I would sit
on the hill of stones and look down
on the trees, on the lake
far away with its boats and those
who ride in boats
and I could not pray. Some of us
have mule minds,
are foolish as sails whipping
in the wind, senseless
as sheets rolling through the fields,

some of us are not given
even a wheel of the tinker's cart
upon which to pray.
When I came back I pumped water
in the yard under the trees
by the fence where the cows came up,
but water is not wisdom
and change is not made by wishes.
Else I would have ridden something,
even a mule, over
those hills and away.

The Cruel Mother

Seven years a fish you'll be.
Seven years a bird in a tree.
Seven years to ring a bell.
Seven years the porter of hell.

The Cruel Mother (a folk ballad)

i. the pool

The thorn at my back a soft hand, so sharp
my cry, the caterwaul of a cat, its belly
sewn with rocks. . . . and then there was nothing,
and then there were two babes tolling
the sand and scarlet marbling the shallow
water I had brought myself to, step by step.
The rose willow dropped soiled catkins. I
could not remember the road to my father's
house.
          Around my waist
my aunt, smelling of emollient, wrapped
white silk—*a man will love you best of all*—
I was small, my hair was fair. Together
when my uncle died, we scrubbed his mealy
skin, picked onion from his teeth, tied
ribbons around his wrists and ankles
so that he could not walk abroad, could not
rattle his traps in our sleep; but at night,
when I lay in the sweat and powder, the
glove of my aunt's breasts, I heard steps,
three by three, by thirty three, and smelled
sour milk: nothing can be kept from where
it wants to be.
          Still, I have bound
twine around these hands too, have with such
slight insult—the sweet crimson slit of
a fish's mouth—emptied these bellies of
prayer. That is a good thing. What sounds
where it does not belong brings confusion.
A good thing. Though among the blown ferns

on the path there was this morning a dead
sparrow, covered with maggots; and now the
carp have grown still and hang in the water
like eyes.

ii. the wall

Under the lolling guelder rose there
was a cow, berried thick with flies, its
heavy sacs swinging like bells. I filled
my tin cup with sweet milk and held it
out to the little girl—the cream made
a satin bow around her mouth; but as I
watched, it turned brown. She smiled and
put her ribboned foot on mine and said,
"I hate you." What had I done? The boy
was jerking his thumb at me, and someone
was watching behind the wall.

iii. the punishment

The fen is frozen, plantain dead,
in the bitter air the coarse grasses grieve.
Lonely cranes hiss and leave. We carp
are not eyes at all, but tongues,
the cauled pool's dumb tongues, telling the same
sad story again and again—
that what begins in brackish waters
comes to a butcher's end.

* * * *

I, the sparrow, sing what is lost
is lost is less than my nest
above the bog where the fat red roots
drag and dissolve. None
of my eggs hatch; the cuckoo robs
me yearly, spilling yolk over the white straw.
You were a keen bird as I remember,
as I remember less and less.

* * * * *

We ring the bells, we with the knotted limbs
and sour smells ring the bells
to frighten the children away. The flesh
is a shallow well: into the dark
we drop our buckets, but bring up nothing.

* * * * *

At this door I have learned to stand still,
to count footfall as coins: *a thousand*
years are as yesterday now that it is past
or as a watch in the night. The woman
with hair like a thrush's breast and rose perfume
came in with a different man tonight,
her finger like a petal on his arm, her smile
a crimson wing; he bowed low to her. I
would not for the world again
have such a fine shoe upon my foot.

The White Deer

The sister was mad
and so must be forgiven,
mad as the deer
trapped in the cow field,
over and again
it threw itself at the fences,
leaping in that leaping
that is not running but flight,
bloodying its mouth,
bloodying its chest,
four blood spots
like hand prints on its neck,
frenzied by those
who helpless would yet help it,
the man and his wife
flapping like large birds
veering this way and that
to head it to the gate,
while the hawk and its thirst
flew low over the cornfield,
flew low toward the promise
of the deer hanging high,
high on the fence
with its head dropped down,
like the hand of a girl
who has given it all up,
who has looked to the sky
and to those who would help her
and has laid her soft head
on the ground.

Part III

The Teacher

Still, still, still, the raven
flies up. His fingered
wings wagging as Mr. Foley's fingers
wag at the children. And he old in his teeth.
And he old in his knees. And knowing little
and helping no one. Only his fingers
wagging like a curtain going up
and a curtain going down.

In the low field
the cow with no hair on her knees
walks backwards under the locust tree. And the boy
Mr. Foley pointed at with his many fingers
waits for her. Stands in the flop
and waits, his hands full of powder
to free her of flies.

Mr. Foley killed this boy.
Or was it the bird? Or was Mr. Foley
the bird? The bird who broke
the boy's knees? The boy
wept in his hair. In his arm.
So ashamed, so lonely, without water or clothes.

Still, still, still, the willow
says forgive. The boy
may be planted in the field. Perhaps
he will grow like a fence or a tree
and the tent worms will build him their nests—
string their white wings
from his heart, from his heels,
and he will be halfway
to heaven and up.

Imagining Their Own Hymns

What fools they are to believe the angels
in this window are in ecstasy. They
do not smile. Their eyes are rolled back in annoyance
not in bliss, as my mother's eyes roll back
when she finds us in the dirt with the cider—
flies and juice blackening our faces and hands.
When the sun comes up behind the angels
then even in their dun robes they are beautiful,
with their girlish hair and their mean lit faces,
but they do not love the light. As I
do not love it when I am made clean
for the ladies who bring my family money.
They stroke my face and smooth my hair. So sweet,
they say, so good, but I am not sweet or good.
I would take one of the possums we kill
in the dump by the woods where the rats slide
like dark boats into the dark stream and leave it
on the heavy woman's porch just to think
of her on her knees scrubbing and scrubbing
at a stain that will never come out.
And these angels that the women turn to
are not good either. They are sick of Jesus,
who never stops dying, hanging there white
and large, his shadow blue as pitch, and blue
the bruise on his chest, with spread petals,
like the hydrangea blooms I tear from
Mrs. Macht's bush and smash on the sidewalk.
One night they will get out of here. One night
when the weather is turning cold and a few
candles burn, they will leave St. Blase standing
under his canopy of glass lettuce
and together, as in a wedding march,
their pockets full of money from the boxes
for the sick poor, they will walk down the aisle,

imagining their own hymns, past the pews
and the water fonts in which small things float,
down the streets of our narrow town, while
the bells ring and the birds fly up in the fields
beyond—and they will never come back.

The Leaving

My father said I could not do it,
but all night I picked the peaches.
The orchard was still, the canals ran steadily.
I was a girl then, my chest its own walled garden.
How many ladders to gather an orchard?
I had only one and a long patience with lit hands
and the looking of the stars which moved right through me
the way the water moved through the canals with a voice
that seemed to speak of this moonless gathering
and those who had gathered before me.
I put the peaches in the pond's cold water,
all night up the ladder and down, all night my hands
twisting fruit as if I were entering a thousand doors,
all night my back a straight road to the sky.
And then out of its own goodness, out
of the far fields of the stars, the morning came,
and inside me was the stillness a bell possesses
just after it has been rung, before the metal
begins to long again for the clapper's stroke.
The light came over the orchard.
The canals were silver and then were not,
and the pond was—I could see as I laid
the last peach in the water—full of fish and eyes.

Napa Valley

Sacks of hair swing on the trees still,
    though my uncle has left this house,
this hill, left the vines that fix
whatever they find to the ground
    as they go.

Five years he swept the barber's floor,
    while the streets darkened, long after
the barber's door closed—five years, up
on this hill, under the swinging lamps
    while the filled pots

smoldered and fumed, he'd tie the golden hair,
    the black, the gray, to the fruit trees
to frighten the deer away. Strange fruit,
strange fruit full of strange seed. As the deer
    believe. As we

believe, locking our saints' bones
    in cathedrals, in stone caskets, and praying
for their ghosts to put a pox on whatever
eats our small homes. *Catch us*
    the little foxes

that spoil our vineyards, for our vineyards
    are in blossom, our vineyards,
with their oily fires, are open to the dark,
to the eyes, to the ochre bodies that rise
    from the hill's

ochre crown and come down as thieves
    to make the valley their own.
So we deck the vines, bauble the trees—that
each might bring fruit in its time:
    oranges lighting

the morning, as if every fine day the child
        were born; green grapes turning
to sun; olives heavy with their sacks of oil.
But what the deer cannot spoil,
        the rains will.

This hill slips. The vines turn black
        or fall. My uncle moves to another hill,
with a house under walnut trees. No vines,
no vines at all. No oranges falling
        like luck

to the dry ground. Though still, at night
        when the trees and the high winds
close around his house, my uncle walks.
His hands are empty now. The town flashes below.
        My uncle walks

in the night. The night heron calls back
        from the lagoon. He walks
in the night and watches for Orion, owls,
the Bear—whatever else might fall
        through the air.

Mount Angel

All up that steep road the pines
leaned on the sky's scaffold—shields
tipped against a wall, light from a dying
fire playing their surfaces—and at the top
lay the monastery—an old dog asleep on
the flagstones—pig squall rising from
the monks' farm; Annie, in lace, braving
the mud, the stench, to wave her white
hand over the huge bristled snouts, croon
lullabies to what she assumed was misunder-
stood. When the priest spoke, it was of apostasy,
of adultery—the holy water turned to ice
in the fonts, rows of fathers nodded in their bone
collars, and someone dumped a bucket of blood
in the well; but I tell you, I have lost many
things, and what he said was nothing to me, was
as innocuous as the rosary of plastic peonies
propped by the lily-smothered pond on that
high hill—so sure was I of the crown
of rain falling over the flowers, the stone
benches, the fields far below where the Old
Believers, haloed with strawberry moths, bent
and picked fruit beside the ancient convent
full of nuns brooding over sad brooms, collecting
the prayers rattling down from the monastery
so that nothing might be lost. No one
had to tell me the graveyard was less
than it seemed, the huge white Christ,
placid as lard above the wooden crosses, one
grave open, ready for the crippled nun who
would not die, to do so; nor did Annie need
to turn in the silence after the sermon
while the incense fell like rain and say,
"I hear it. I feel the stroke of the passing
bell."

Christmas Eve, Old People's Guild, Mt. Angel

As light dissolves like new snow
                    over the day bread
and moldy prunes sold by the old people
in Mt. Angel, a boy balancing
                    bags of oranges
on his handlebars disappears
down the monastery drive
between shadows and the broken stations
                    of the cross; I turn,
a man in a caftan smiles, *he will take*
my money, I think, *he will do*
                    bad things to me, and
a woman with patched skin
puts coins on the counter; she is cheerful
                    pushing her lower lip
like a christmas sausage out
                    for the dog, and I,
with my handmade socks, hold back, not standing
too close, though I am ashamed,
there is much wrong with me already:

                    but others are laughing and clinking
                    their coffee spoons, spilling sugar on card
                    tables, and beside trays
                                        of fudge the stuffed monkey
                    claps his cymbals—O we will be good, good
                    and not afraid,
                    we will keep ourselves in lavender and clove
                    like woolen scarves in Nana's drawers,
                    we will not think of darkness; the windows—
                    painted with pictures of storks
                                        and kings, sacks of coins—
                    are ours, they say we can stay
                    always in this room
                    with the wooden man and his sheep, carved cribs
                    and ruby rum, cheeses

                      shaped like bells, gold
        and brass balls spinning round in our hands.

Down the street through the snow
                 the old druggist, his
glasses slipping, chases my friend, calling
and waving the bottle of aspirin
                he has found for her at last
behind the teething biscuits and the salt,
behind those small rings
children break their gums on.

The Hill

(for Huck)

When the dog barks at nothing,
when the heat lightning
makes its phantoms in the sky—those
  who are passing, those who are passing,
        wearing their robes,

        even they have their hungers—
then you by the gate
have no power to harm me. I shall go out
  as the crickets do
        with the frost, letting

        their lake of sound
thin to ice. I shall go out
and this field will no longer be mine
  where one poplar stands
        and the archer's target draws

        the night's invisible arrows down,
draws down the stars. They fall
into the target as into the sea
  and so we are born
        and so shall die

        on this hill or elsewhere
and pass over this hill
or elsewhere, lighting the sky
  when it is hot and the flesh remembers
        its songs.

I will trust the dream.
My son holds the arrow
in his hand, holds time to its target
   and its grief,
         and time like lightning

      will split the shaft,
leaving this land to others—
                  and him to me.

The House on Main Street

If we had bought the house on Main Street I wanted,
  across from the Shoe Repair Shop
    where the five-bulbed lamp stands
always lit in the window behind the Bilt-rite and Cat's
    Paw signs, I would know now
  who died, know for whom the gray hearse glided

to a delicate stop this morning before the broad red doors
  of the Presbyterian Church, know
    why the whole town was there singing
inside. Where we live on our hill only the deer
    congregate, thin as air, the ghosts
  of lost soldiers, trailing torn flags, as they look

for the deaths they left under the tall pines. But if
  we had bought that house, and could
    begin this day again, then I could early watch
a hundred cars come to town, watch them fill
    the macadam beneath the hoop the town
  kids pound the ball against until their fingers

bleed, cheered on by the Insurance Company's secretary
  and the bevies of pigeons preening
    on the old factory which almost
burned this winter, when Mr. Yeakel's youngest son—who
    thought the town's firemen would surely, if
  they saw him put a fire out, hire him—set

fire to the green garage beside it, and then raised
  the alarm, as alarms were raised
    all year for fires that took stores
and animals, and during the big storm, three
    children's lives. But say again
  that we live on Main Street and it is early

and I can watch the cars pull up beside the charred
    Oldsmobile that still stands where
        the green garage stood, watch the children
poke the bag of clothespins bulging like a wasps' nest
    on the Hanson's umbrella line, watch
        cars block Bridge Street, where, on the steps

of a house the Catholics converted into a church by
    fitting it with green glass and sprinkling
        it with holy water, and which now belongs
to the Mormons, two girls in shorts and lipstick and much-
    arranged hair sit and stare
        at the window behind which the dead man lies. (In whom,

we forget, death has now no interest. But see how
    death is there, touching this man,
        then that, the feathers of a flowered
hat, the preacher's thin hair.) Say I sit
    in our window on Main Street
        and count the people getting out in front

of the latticework propped beside the Shoe Repair Shop
    whose dilapidated face
        made my husband afraid to buy
this house; and say the two fat men who in warm
    weather sun themselves on
        the collapsing porch above the shop come out

with their beer. Say this, for this is why I wanted
    to live here, on Main Street,
        to see what hours those men
like to sit in the sun, to watch down the street
    people passing under the swinging
        tooth-shaped sign and into the dentist's office

of Doctor Joseph Grow, whose beautiful hydrangeas now
    dangle decayed balls over
        the porch rail, to stand
in our yard next to the rusted road sign that points
        West to Portland and the Water
Gap, South to Hope; and this is why I write here

what I write, recalling a funeral to which I was not
    invited, for which the town
        library closed in respect, while
my overdue books sat on the truck's seat and
        baked in the sun that warmed
        that gray hearse, warmed that newly dug hole

in the cemetery, that saw—five years ago among the cedars
    while the cows grazed unperturbed
        in the pines beyond the spear-
barred cemetery rails—a vagrant girl, about
        whom they are now making a movie,
        murdered; the cemetery I stare at so often

from our Bank, watching the small flags flap
    and whistle, watching men
        shovel dirt, watching the keeper
monthly haul dead wreathes and pile them before
        the gate, watching the day
        my daughter and I ran among the stones

with our dog, who rudely peed on many graves, ran there
    together for want of another
        place, in this state where No
Trespassing signs are nailed everywhere, as they were
        not in the wide midwestern
        farmland where I grew up, and one could walk

for miles and miles and never cross a marked fence,
    or hear the heavy tread
        of hunters, or see their bright
guns. It was sunny the day we ran, though
        still winter. It is hard
    to find a home. The earth is not stable beneath

our feet. We slip on the icy grass, our hands
    full of the strange coarsely spotted
        feathers we pick up among
the stones and wish upon, as if by gripping
        them in our palms, or
    stuffing them in our coats, we can be

connected with flight, not with the stone angels
    shadowing the frozen
        ground, but with a body
that has truly flown, with a mind
        that makes the sky
its home.

epilogue

I walk later in the cemetery
to find out who has died, needing to know,
but there are five graves newly filled—
the sweet sour smell of flowers rotting
in their toppled jars heavy on the air.
Alta T. Sprague is here, Frank Hunt, and
Albert Yetter. Under a carved lamb
lies good Earnest Rea; and at the feet
of Ellen T., whose last name is hidden
by a styrofoam Virgin stuck with red
and white carnations and bound by wire
to her marble stone, a bright flag flaps.
These at least are in their graves, unlike
the animals supposedly buried in
our famous pet cemetery which, it turns out,

were never under their fancy markers at all
but had been thrown behind the lake
into huge pits that poisoned all the wells
along Willow Run with their decay.
It grows warm then cold. Along the roads
possums fall beneath our tires. Some years
are years for dying, as they are for fire.

Part IV

Those Who Wrestle With the Angel For Us

(for Dion)

i.

My brother flies
A plane,
       windhover, night-lover,
Flies too low
Over the belled
       and furrowed fields,
The coiled creeks,
The slow streams of cars
       spilling
Like lust into the summer
Towns. And he flies
       when he
Should not, when
The hot, heavy air
       breaks
In storms, in high
Winds, when the clouds
       like trees
Unload their stony fruit
And batter his slender
       wings and tail.
But like the magician's
Dove, he appears home safely
       every time,
Carrying in his worn white
Bag all the dark
       elements
That flight knows,
The dark that makes
       his own soul
Dark with sight.

Even when he was a child, his skin was the white
Of something buffed by winds at high altitudes

Or lit by arctic lights—it gleamed like fish scales
Or oiled tin, and even then he wished to be alone,

Disappearing into the long grasses of the Ipperwash dunes
Where the gulls nested and where one afternoon

He fell asleep and was almost carried off by the sun—
In his dream he was running, leaping well, leaping

High as the hunted deer, and almost leaping free,
But like the tide, my gentle-handed mother hauled him back

With cold compresses and tea, and after that he favored
The dark, the ghostly hours, a small boy whistling in our yard

As he dragged a stick along the fence rails, and listened
To the slatted rattle of railroad cars, and knew by

Instinct how railroad lines look from the air, like ladders
Running northward to the stars, to the great constellations.

And he began then tracking his way through the names
Of all our fears, Cassiopeia, Andromeda, the shining Ram,

Tracking the miles and years he logs now, the lonely stretches
Where he finds the souvenirs that light our narrow kitchens—

Buckles and pins, watches and rings—the booty
That makes our land-locked, land-bound souls feel the compass

In our feet, and see in those who never speak, who
Slouch in with the dust of the northern wind on their backs,

The face of the angel we ourselves must wrestle with.

Given the River

The falcon's eye is always
open. He holds the crow
with his foot and plucks the black
feathers out. Some of us
would eat crow rather
than give in. Some of us
want nothing of wine.
                    The cicadas
rattle the heat with their
castanets, calling a Christ home
or wishing one, building up
and up and letting go,
thinking No, not this one,
not this, *how long must we sing?*
And Christ walks in.
This may be so. There was a fox
in the cornfield redder
than the corn and he was running
the show—pulling scarves
from his heels and making
the dust bow. He ate stones
pretending they were teeth
and many, and his belly
full of ivory and no one
to stop him.
                The hallways
in the corn are dark and close
and they lead always
to the river, which is also dark
and close and full of red
fish rising, full of desire
for the cellars of the houses,
and the sweet fruits
that sleep there, and the good jam.

Above the Quarry

The cocks cry *death death* each morning
But the death they cry is orange-feathered
And slathered over with sun—not

The foolish, lame-legged death you creep
After, looking behind cupboard and stove.
Death should be worn like a feathered cape.

It should be found in the highest oaks
Or in the damp hay rows of a morning where
The steep fields that the farmer plows

Precariously in spring, far away, soundlessly
Turning over gold row after gold row,
Climb above the pit. And like the fevered dog

It should run. *O death,* says the hawk,
Is mine, those of us who eat rocks know
The rocks' tongue, the salt and the lime,

Know that a rope swings above the shadowy
Water of the pit, a rope for girls to leap
Over, or for men to tie knots in, or

For the soul to slide down when it wishes
To breast like the swallows the blue body of doubt
And swing beyond it to the hill where

Those harp-winged birds guard and feed
Their young: that hill where your sorrow stands—
Like the fence row, fragile to the wind,

Leaf-tattered, wood-tattered, and grim. And
It is that hill you must love, that sodden,
mulched and blackened late autumn hill where

The wings that rise rise as dark flags
Toward a sun which is pewter and cold as
The water pooling in the lowest depths

Of the pit; that hill you must stare into,
Knowing that if a soul can recognize itself
In one time, one season, one hour of one day,

Then it can walk as through a mirror
Past itself, and begin . . . Listen, the dog barks,
The dead deer come back in flocks to teach

The new deer their paths, and the fog thickens.
You are wading in the water singing songs,
The water is loosening your clothes, and you

Are not warm but cold and glad at the chill
Thrill that lights your bones and puts
So many wildly feathered caps upon your head,

So many beaks within your palm.

The Visitation

God sends his tasks
and one does
them or not, but the sky
delivers its gifts
at the appointed
times: With spit and sigh,
with that improbable
burst of flame, the balloon
comes over
the cornfield, bringing
another country
with it, bringing
from a long way off
those colors that are at first
the low sound
of a horn, but soon
are many horns, and clocks,
and bells, and clappers
and your heart
rising to the silence
in all of them, a silence
so complete that
the heads of the corn
bow back before it
and the dog flees in terror
down the road
and you alone are left
gazing up
at three solemn visitors
swinging
in a golden cage
beneath that unbelievable chorus of red
and white, swinging
so close you cannot move

or speak, so close
the road grows wet with light,
as when the sun flares
after an evening storm
and you become weightless, falling
back in the air
before the giant oak
that with a fiery burst
the balloon
just clears.

The Place of Trumpets

To the place of trumpets,
To the place where the sun sets,
To the place where peace sits,

We are going. By twos
Or threes, going to choose
New weather and new clothes,

The new sound of words walking
As trees among the winging
Fields, the fields on herons' wings;

Where all who wake, wake undone,
Back beyond their fragile bones,
Back to where the self is song,

Where the unmade hands are wheels,
The arms newest prayer shawls,
And the heart the child that kneels

And never tires, and never
Fails to watch at the door
The sun plucking its poor

Chest open and scattering
Its blood out, dropping
Down its bloody lasting blessing.

To the place of trumpets
We are going. To the sweet
Beggar's pipes blowing and wet

Winds unwinding the last
Winding sheets on streets where past
And present meet, where West

Marries East, and trust turns
To betrayal as its friend,
Where days and moon and sins are one

Blessed wind passing over
The passing plains, over
The sea, the comforter,

Full of salt so sweet it fills
The hollow tongue until
It splits as time will

Split and spill its tattered toys,
Fixed by the merest gaze
Or longing in the place

Where quiet ways grow,
Where the wound loves the arrow,
Where ankle and adder know

Accord, where the lion's lamb
Leads him to the grasses down,
Leads him with her little song,

Lay us here, lay us long,
Let us in this grass as one
Sleep now where we first began,

Here on the sand where we first met,
Under the trees before His seat,
Out of the cold, out of the heat,

In the place of trumpets.

To the Lost Child

(for Anna)

This is the field you did not come to, this
the damp November day confederate
clouds trail defeat across. The far hills
are purple as the ashes of old fires,
and black as guns or crutches the trees. But the fields
are oddly green, still, in this winter thaw.
Or perhaps it is late fall—the small
measures we find ourselves with
don't change the movement of things. We, like this crow,
passing over the cedars in lazy,
widening circles, wobbling and sliding
as it rights itself by some internal decree,
can only ride the currents that *are,*
and are not held, up and down.
                                        I am glad
of the crows, they are like my own hands,
always here, always remembering the day
to itself, glad of the trees, of the startling
red weeds and blue pools of shale
in this field where one tulip poplar stands
brisk and tall as a good child, a bee box
at her feet, a bee box full of humming.
And this humming is the maker, the body
of the gold it broods over. This must be so.
Pollen would have no savor if it came
from colorless flowers, and silent bees,
for all their flying, would make no honey
but some watery substance, or nothing
at all. For sound does make things happen.
The cows wander and when they cry
I heave hay, rank with mold and the months
of dust that fly up in blue clouds, over
the fence; the red-hatted hunter shouts
and the deer careers into or away from

the arrow's whistling arc; planes moan,
the head rises to heaven. And, Anna,
had you called as our bull calf Moses did,
all night when he was first new, tied to a pine
under the window, bullying the thin air
he found himself in, wailing at the cows
on the other side of the fence
who would not see him for what he was
until he forgot what he was and thought
we were one of him and he a fine man
in his uniform—had you called you would
have brought the sweet milk trickling between
your lips to form its lovely, cloudy pool.
I will not be sad. I count the things
I put in a box for us, all I thought
you would see, the scrawny forsythia starters—
pulled from the mother plant that smothers
the gate and each year must be thinned—tottering
along the drive, the deer trail lined
with the yellow roses that are still foolishly
blooming, the pines that cut the gray sky,
and the brilliant burning bush that, all improbably,
Moses, then grown, ate most of
before he barrelled away through the woods
to the farmer's far barley field, where, proud and stupid,
he ate his fill until we took
him away to one whose sturdy fences
would keep him home.

              I can sit for a long
time now. Some war is over. Below me
the bog in the woods is black
and pungent with decay and the oil from
the red cans the old tenant left, and below that,
at the base of the hill, the rushing stream
is a gathering of voices. Many voices.
Yours. Mine. It moves, we move, and hands,

these things that find and belong
to each other, also move and carry like water
more than themselves, as they fly in their bird-
like ways toward whatever small purposes
they have been given.

Lullaby for the Gardener

(for John Witte)

If you fall from the apple tree
Because your glasses fall before you,

Because your sight lies lost on the ground
And your hand reaches after it—

Do not fear. The ground for all its thorny branches
Will gather you. The espaliered pears

Your hands in their sight tied back
As patiently as they tied your daughter's braids

Will hum their pinioned lullaby,
And your heart, which is a purple fruit, will burst

To become the fire your braided daughter feeds.
Do not fear. Beneath her feet

The orchard dirt is black and soft,
And the branch she holds is more than a staff.

When she strikes the ground
It will open. Blue in the blue dusk

The horses will gather, and the soldiers who love them
Will lift lit tapers. The orchard will turn

As the stars turn, and you, standing
In the stream, will see that the moon you fear

Is both your daughter's armor
And the voice that will lead her like a reckless lover

Wherever she would not go—through brambles
And thickets, wildwoods and fens,

And when the day fails, into the flames,
Where the moon will become

For her darkening limbs: the water you stand in,
The arms you hold out,

The fare for the last crossing of all.

CPSIA information can be obtained
at www.ICGtesting.com
Printed in the USA
BVHW051417080922
646450BV00004B/653